UNEXPLAINED

DISAPPEARANCES

Rupert Matthews

QED Publishing

Project Editor: Paul Manning/White-Thomson Publishing
Designer: Tim Mayer/White-Thomson Publishing
Picture Researcher: Maria Joannou

First published in the UK in 2010 by
QED Publishing
A Quarto Group Company
226 City Road
London EC1V 2TT

www.qed-publishing.co.uk

ISBN 978-1-84835-366-4

Printed and bound in China

Picture credits
Key: t=top, b=bottom, r=right, l=left, c=centre

**The words in bold are explained in
the Glossary on page 30.**

You can find the answers
to the questions asked on
these notebooks on page 31.

CONTENTS

This book describes some of the most baffling and mysterious disappearances of all time. Many of them have remained unsolved for centuries.

ASKING QUESTIONS

When people or things suddenly vanish, it is natural to ask questions – and often there is a simple explanation. Maybe a crime has been committed, or an accident of some kind has taken place.

Since the 1950s many mysterious disappearances have taken place in the stretch of ocean known as the Bermuda Triangle in the western North Atlantic.

But sometimes people vanish in **bizarre** circumstances, and there are no clues to what happened – or the clues that are left behind just add to the mystery. Occasionally, an entire ship will vanish without trace, or an aircraft will take off and never be seen again.

 The British explorer Percy Fawcett disappeared in the 1920s while searching for a lost city in the jungles of Brazil.

DISTRESS SIGNALS

Usually ships or aircrafts that get into difficulties send out distress signals – but not always. When a DC4 airliner disappeared over Lake Michigan during a routine flight from New York to Seattle on 23 June 1950, no call for help was ever received. Debris was later found floating in the water, but the wreckage of the plane itself has never been found.

Just as baffling is the case of the three lighthouse keepers who disappeared on the remote Scottish island of Eilean Mohr. Inside the lighthouse, everything had been left in perfect order. The **logbook** had been kept up to date and there was no sign of anything wrong. Yet the men vanished without trace and were never seen again.

Lake Michigan in North America has been the scene of several unexplained incidents involving ships and planes.

How many answers to famous unsolved mysteries lie at the bottom of the sea?

THE LOST PATROL

Over the last 60 years, the area of ocean known as the Bermuda Triangle has been the scene of many strange disappearances. One of the most mysterious was the case of Flight 19.

The legendary 'lost squadron', Flight 19, believed lost in the Bermuda Triangle shortly after the end of the Second World War.

DISAPPEARANCE FILE

Subject Flight 19
Date 5 December 1945
Place Coast of Florida, USA
Status UNEXPLAINED

LOST AT SEA

On 5 December 1945, a flight of five US Avenger torpedo bombers took off from Fort Lauderdale Air Force base in Florida, USA. The pilots were due to carry out a routine practice bombing attack at sea.

After the planes had completed the practice, the flight commander, Lieutenant Charles Carroll Taylor, exchanged several routine radio messages with base. But then his messages became stranger. Shortly afterwards, all contact was lost. The planes were never seen again.

This Avenger **torpedo** bomber is similar to the planes flown by the pilots of Flight 19. The Avenger was sturdy, easy to fly and popular with pilots.

WHAT REALLY HAPPENED?

The truth about Flight 19 will probably never be known. The official story was that the planes simply got lost and ditched in the sea. One theory is that unusual 'magnetic forces' in the Bermuda Triangle may have interfered with compasses and other equipment on board the planes.

NO SURVIVORS

As soon as the aircraft were reported missing, a search was mounted. Aircraft and ships in the area were asked to watch out for wreckage and survivors. Nothing was ever found.

WHAT HAPPENED NEXT?

The US Navy launched an investigation. It was found that after the bombing practice, the planes had headed northeast to the Bahamas, but that for some reason, the flight commander had thought they were heading south west to the Florida Keys. Instead of returning to Florida, in fact he led the planes further out to sea. The report could not explain how he made such a basic mistake. It concluded with the words 'Cause Unknown'.

Who commanded Flight 19?

What type of plane were the pilots flying?

What were the final words of the Navy's report?

LOST AT SEA

When a big ship goes down, investigators can often piece together the story of what happened by studying the wreckage. But if a vessel vanishes without trace, the mystery can remain unsolved forever.

DISAPPEARANCE FILE

Subject   USS Cyclops
Date   March 1918
Place   North Atlantic Ocean
Status   UNEXPLAINED

One such case was the USS *Cyclops*, a 17,000-tonne **cargo** ship owned by the US Navy. Sometime after 4 March 1918, the ship vanished while carrying a cargo of **ore** from Rio de Janeiro in Brazil to Baltimore, Maryland, on the east coast of the USA.

All 306 of the ship's passengers and crew disappeared without trace. The Navy had lost warships in battle before, but it was very unusual for so many lives to be lost so mysteriously.

Some believe that the USS *Cyclops'* huge cargo of ore made her **unstable** and that she sank in a heavy storm.

DISTURBING

At the time the Cyclops vanished, the USA was at war with Germany. Some believed the ship could have been 'stolen' by its German-born captain and handed over to the enemy.

After the search for the missing ship began, the US Navy received a disturbing **telegram** from a US official in Barbados, sent before the Cyclops went missing. According to the official, the ship's captain had taken on a lot of extra coal and food, as if he was preparing for a long voyage. The official also said that many of the passengers had German names. His message ended: "I fear a fate worse than sinking."

This crew member was one of 236 officers and men who are believed to have lost their lives when the USS Cyclops disappeared.

How many people were on board the USS Cyclops when it vanished?

What nationality was the ship's captain?

What was the ship carrying when it vanished?

WHAT REALLY HAPPENED?

One theory, supported by the Barbados telegram, is that German passengers took over the Cyclops, killed the crew and sailed to Germany. But after the war ended, the Germans denied all knowledge of the ship. Many other theories have been suggested, but none that really solves the mystery.

In 1937, American pilot Amelia Earhart set off to become the first woman to fly around the world. It was a journey from which she never returned.

Aged 40, Amelia Earhart was an outstanding pilot who broke many flying records. Before her disappearance, both she and her navigator Fred Noonan had successfully completed many long flights.

EMPTY OCEAN

Just after midnight on 2 July, Earhart took off from Lae in New Guinea on one of the final stages of her journey. She was bound for Howland Island, a tiny strip of land in the middle of the Pacific, where a US coastguard ship, the *Itasca*, was waiting to guide her in.

Early that morning, the *Itasca* picked up a radio message from Earhart saying that she could not find Howland Island. After this, the signals from Earhart's Electra 10E plane became fainter and fainter. Then there was silence.

DISAPPEARANCE FILE

Subject	Amelia Earhart
Date	2 July 1937
Place	Pacific Ocean
Status	UNEXPLAINED

OUT OF FUEL

At first, people thought that Earhart had run out of fuel and crashed into the sea. Then the radio signals were **analyzed**. One seemed to come from Gardner Island, about 500 kilometres south of Howland. Later, the island was searched, and a skeleton, a woman's shoe and a piece of **aluminium**, possibly from an aircraft, were found.

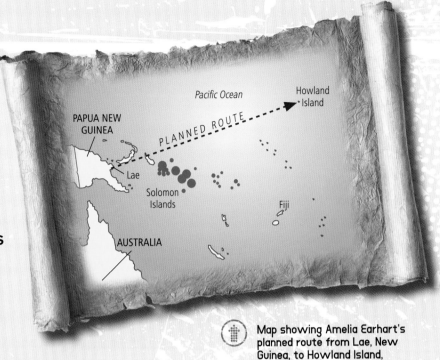

Map showing Amelia Earhart's planned route from Lae, New Guinea, to Howland Island, halfway between Australia and Hawaii, USA.

WHAT REALLY HAPPENED?

Some have claimed that Earhart crash-landed on Japanese-occupied Saipan Island, and was later executed as a US spy. However, photographs showing Earhart as a prisoner turned out to be fake. Others believe Earhart is still alive somewhere under another name, but there is no evidence to support this.

Over the years, many theories were put forward to explain Amelia Earhart's disappearance, but nothing was ever found that could be proved to be from her plane. Her case remains one of the great unsolved mysteries of the twentieth century.

What type of aircraft was Earhart flying?

Who was Earhart's navigator?

Which island was Earhart heading for when she vanished?

THE LOST COLONY

In sixteenth-century America, many **settlers** lost their lives in the struggle to build a future in the 'New World'. But could a whole community of 115 people really disappear without leaving any trace?

ON ROANOKE ISLAND

In 1585, English settlers arrived to found a colony on Roanoke, a small island off the coast of North Carolina. Life was hard, and the small community suffered many setbacks. But when the colony's governor left and returned three years later, he was shocked by what he found. Everyone had gone. The houses were empty, and the paths overgrown with weeds. The only clue to what had happened was a single word, 'CROATOAN', carved on a wooden post.

This reconstruction of an early English settlers' village in Virginia shows how the Roanoke colony might have looked.

DISAPPEARANCE FILE
Subject   The Lost Colony of Roanoke
Date   1587
Place   Roanoke, Virginia
Status   UNEXPLAINED

WHAT REALLY HAPPENED?

*One possibility is that the settlers ran out of food, tried to return to England but died on the journey. More likely, the survivors ended up living among nearby Native American tribes, who either adopted or **enslaved** them. Scientists and historians are now testing this theory.*

'CROATOAN'

Before he left, the governor had told the settlers that if anything went wrong, they were to leave a clue to what had happened. If they went to live with the nearby, friendly Croatoan tribe, they were to write 'CROATOAN' on a tree. If they were attacked or driven out against their will, they were to carve a cross instead.

For years afterwards, people tried to find out what had happened. Some reported seeing fair-skinned people on nearby Croatoan Island. Others reported seeing traces of settlements further along the North Carolina coast. To this day, no one can say for certain what happened to the Roanoke settlers.

 Archaeologists **excavate** the site of a fort close to where the original Roanoke colony is believed to have stood.

When was the Roanoke colony founded?

How many colonists disappeared?

What word was found carved on a post at Roanoke?

On 26 July 1909, the luxury steamer SS *Waratah* set sail from Durban in South Africa with 211 passengers and crew. Built to carry passengers emigrating from Europe to Australia, the *Waratah* was returning to England after her second voyage.

BRIGHT FLASHES

On the 27 July, a ship called the *Harlow* spotted a large steamer that looked like the *Waratah* some distance away. Later, the crew of the *Harlow* saw two bright flashes on the horizon, but they thought they were caused by fires on the shore.

The *Waratah* was due to reach Cape Town on 29 July. She never arrived. Naval ships searched the area where she was last seen, but no trace of her was ever found.

DISAPPEARANCE FILE

Subject	SS Waratah
Date	27 July 1909
Place	Indian Ocean
Status	UNEXPLAINED

Known as the 'Australian *Titanic*', the SS *Waratah* was only one year old at the time of her disappearance. The ship did not carry a radio, but this was not unusual at the time.

PUBLIC ENQUIRY

After the *Waratah* disappeared, a public enquiry was held in London. Some experts said the ship might have been top-heavy; others said she could have been the victim of a freak wave or a 'hole in the ocean', when winds and currents can drag even a large ship to the bottom.

Many theories were argued back and forth. The well-known writer of the *Sherlock Holmes* stories, Sir Arthur Conan Doyle, even held a **séance** to try and find out what had happened. But in the end, no one could explain how such a large ship could vanish without leaving either wreckage or survivors.

WHAT REALLY HAPPENED?

The Waratah *was carrying a heavy cargo of lead which could have shifted, causing her to capsize. But if so, where was the wreck? In 1999, the wreck of a big ship was spotted in the area where the* Waratah *vanished, but this was found to be a transport ship sunk by a German* **U-boat** *in 1942.*

Many ships have been lost in stormy seas off this rocky **headland**, known as the Cape of Good Hope, on the southern tip of South Africa.

How many people were on board the Waratah?

What famous ship was the Waratah compared to?

Which port was the Waratah bound for?

In 1872, a small cargo ship was found drifting in the Atlantic Ocean. Everything on board seemed perfectly normal, except for one thing: the ship was deserted. No trace of the crew has ever been found. The case of the *Mary Celeste* remains one of the great unsolved sea mysteries of all time.

DISAPPEARANCE FILE

Name Mary Celeste
Date November 1872
Place North Atlantic Ocean
Status UNEXPLAINED

SHIP OF GHOSTS

On 5 November 1872, the *Mary Celeste* set sail from New York bound for Genoa in Italy with a valuable cargo of raw alcohol. On board were Captain Benjamin Briggs, his wife and daughter, plus a crew of seven men.

Ten days later, another ship, the *Dei Gratia*, set sail on a similar route under Captain David Morehouse, an acquaintance of Briggs. After a month at sea, Morehouse spotted the *Mary Celeste* drifting in the Atlantic. He immediately sensed that something was wrong and sent his **chief mate**, Oliver Deveau, to investigate. Finding the *Mary Celeste* deserted, Deveau and two others sailed her to Gibraltar.

In a final letter to his mother, the captain of the *Mary Celeste*, Benjamin Briggs, wrote: 'Our vessel is in beautiful trim and I hope we shall have a fine passage.'

WHAT HAPPENED NEXT?

At Gibraltar, an official enquiry was held. The crew of the *Dei Gratia* were questioned and the *Mary Celeste* was examined. All the crew's clothes and possessions were still on board. The cargo was intact. The hatch on the main cargo **hold** was closed, but two smaller hatches were open. The last entry in the log was dated 25 November.

A painting of the *Mary Celeste* in 1861. At this time, the ship was known as the *Amazon*.

WHAT REALLY HAPPENED?

Over the years many people have tried to solve the mystery of the Mary Celeste. *Some even claim the crew were abducted by aliens! One theory is that alcohol fumes from the cargo may have made the captain think the vessel was about to explode, and this was why he and the crew left in such a hurry.*

The enquiry found that Captain Briggs and his crew had abandoned the *Mary Celeste* in a great hurry and taken to the **lifeboat**. Why they had left the ship and what happened to them afterwards was never discovered.

Who was the captain of the Mary Celeste?

What cargo was the Mary Celeste carrying?

Who boarded the Mary Celeste when she was found?

THE LOST ARMY OF CAMBYSES

In the summer of 2000, scientists searching for oil in the Egyptian desert came across weapons, jewellery and human bones buried in the sand. Could these be the remains of the lost army of Cambyses?

After crossing the Sinai desert, Cambyses' army swept into Egypt, easily defeating the forces of Psamtik III at the Battle of Pelusium.

A MIGHTY RULER

In the sixth century BCE, the Persian ruler Cambyses II was one of the most powerful men in the ancient world. After successfully invading Egypt in 525 BCE, Cambyses sent an army of 50,000 soldiers from Thebes to Siwa in the desert west of the River Nile. The soldiers' orders were to attack the Temple of Amun, where rebel priests were refusing to accept his rule.

After marching for seven days across the desert, the army were resting at an **oasis** when a fierce wind sprang up. Soon columns of whirling sand descended on the troops, burying men and animals in clouds of dust.

DISAPPEARANCE FILE

Name	The Lost Army of Cambyses
Date	525 BCE or 524 BCE
Place	Western Egyptian Desert
Status	UNEXPLAINED

 The story of Cambyses' army was first told by the Greek historian, Herodotus (484 –425 BCE).

WHAT HAPPENED NEXT?

Hearing what had happened, Cambyses sent out riders to try to find his army. The trail led through the desert oasis of Bahariya, then southwest toward Siwa, but disappeared in the sand. The huge army had vanished without trace.

For many years, historians thought the story was just a **myth**. But over the last ten years, important finds have been made in Egypt's western desert. These are now being studied by experts. Many believe they could hold the answer to the mysterious fate of Cambyses' army.

WHAT REALLY HAPPENED?

Over the years many explorers and archaeologists have searched in vain for traces of Cambyses' army. The remains found in Egypt recently seem to be of Persian origin, and appear to belong to soldiers who became lost or stranded in the desert. Whether they belong to Cambyses' army is less certain.

When did Cambyses invade Egypt?

Which temple was Cambyses' army planning to attack?

Where have remains of an army been discovered?

Remains of the ancient temple of Amun at Siwa, in the western Egyptian desert.

Eilean Mohr off the west coast of Scotland is one of the most remote islands in the British Isles. According to local legend, it was haunted by ghosts who were determined to drive out intruders. Could this explain the mysterious case of the vanishing lighthousemen?

Eilean Mohr is the largest of the seven rocky Flannan Isles. It rises 87 metres above the Atlantic Ocean, on the west coast of Scotland.

DISAPPEARANCE FILE

Names James Ducat, Thomas Marshall and Donald McArthur

Date December 1900

Place Eilean Mohr, Scotland

Status UNEXPLAINED

DESERTED

On 26 December 1900, lighthouseman Joseph Moore was returning to Eilean Mohr by boat after a fortnight's leave. As Moore approached the island and looked for the usual signs of welcome, he was puzzled to see that there was nobody waiting at the **landing stage** to greet him.

Inside the lighthouse, Moore found the living quarters deserted. On the kitchen table were the remains of a half-eaten meal. An upturned chair lay on the floor. The lighthouse was empty, and its three occupants had disappeared without trace.

WHAT HAPPENED NEXT?

Alarmed, Moore returned with four others to make a full investigation. They discovered that two of the keepers must have left the lighthouse dressed for stormy weather. A third set of oilskins was still hanging on the hook.

The west landing stage had been lashed by gales. A lifebelt had been ripped from its mountings. But no trace was found of the lighthousemen, nor any sign of what could have happened to them. To this day, the mystery of their disappearance remains unsolved.

 The job of the lighthousemen was to keep the lamp lit to guide ships away from the rocks at night.

WHAT REALLY HAPPENED?

Some claim that the three men were carried off by a giant bird or sea creature. It is more likely that during a storm, two of the men went to check the crane on the west landing. Meanwhile, the third man saw big waves approaching and rushed out to warn them. In the confusion, all three were swept out to sea.

When were the disappearances discovered?

Who discovered the disappearances?

How many men disappeared?

On 8 June 1924, British climbers George Mallory and Andrew Irvine set out to conquer Everest – and never came back. Nobody knew what had happened until Mallory's body was discovered in 1999. Could he have been the first man to climb the world's highest mountain?

DISAPPEARANCE FILE

Names George Mallory
Andrew Irvine
Date 8 June 1924
Place Mount Everest, Nepal
Status SOLVED

 At the time of his disappearance Mallory was aged 38 and had many years' experience as a mountaineer. Both he and Irvine were well equipped for climbing at high **altitude**.

IN SIGHT OF VICTORY

On the day that Mallory and Irvine made their fateful attempt on the **summit** of Everest, thick clouds hid the mountain. But for a few minutes around lunchtime, the cloud lifted, and the two men were spotted within sight of the summit. Then they were once more hidden from view. It was the last time they were seen alive.

At 8848 metres, Mount Everest in the Himalayas is the world's highest mountain.

WHAT REALLY HAPPENED?

Many believe that Mallory's attempt on the summit of Everest was successful, and that he died on the way down the mountain. However, there is no proof of this. The fact that the photograph of his wife was not found on his person when his body was discovered in 1999 does not prove that he reached the summit.

MEMORIAL

When Mallory and Irvine failed to come back, their friends waited several days. Then, accepting that they must both have died on the mountain, they built a memorial cairn and left. The mystery of what really happened that day, and whether the two men reached the summit, has never been solved.

These snow goggles, pocket knife and watch were found on Mallory's body in 1999.

WHAT HAPPENED NEXT?

In 1933, Irvine's ice axe was found on a slope at 8500 metres, but there was no sign of his body. It was not until 1999 that Mallory's frozen remains were found 300 metres further down the slope.

Rope marks showed that Mallory had fallen, been caught by the rope and then fallen again. A photo of his wife that he planned to leave on the summit was not in his pocket. Many people took this as a sign that Mallory and Irvine had reached the summit that day and that they were on the way down when the accident occurred.

On what date did Mallory set out for the summit?

When was Mallory's body found?

What did Mallory plan to leave on the summit?

23

DISAPPEARANCE FILE

Subject   Percy Fawcett
Date   June 1925
Place   Mato Grosso, Brazil
Status   UNEXPLAINED

In 1925, the well-known British explorer Percy Fawcett disappeared in mysterious circumstances during an expedition to find an ancient lost city in the jungles of Brazil. His fate and that of his son Jack is still unknown.

LOST CITY

Fawcett was convinced that an ancient lost city that he called 'Z' existed somewhere in the Mato Grosso, a vast wooded region in western Brazil. He left behind strict instructions that, if he did not return, no one should try to rescue him in case they went missing too.

The legendary explorer Percy Fawcett was said to be the inspiration for the film character Indiana Jones.

On 29 May 1925, Fawcett sent a message to his wife that he had reached the Xingu River and was about to enter unexplored territory. The message ended: "You need have no fear of failure". Shortly after this, he headed north into the rainforest. Neither he nor his son Jack was ever seen again.

Map showing the Amazon Basin and the Xingu River region, where Percy Fawcett and his son Jack were last seen.

RUMOURS

After Fawcett disappeared, many rumours started to go around. Some said that Fawcett had been killed by tribespeople or wild animals; others said that Fawcett had lost his memory and was living among **cannibals**.

An explorer called Orlando Villas Boas claimed that Kalapalo tribespeople had confessed to murdering Fawcett and had handed the body over to him. But the bones were later found not to be Fawcett's.

In a BBC interview in 1998, an elder of the Kalapalo denied that the tribe had had any part in Fawcett's death. More than 80 years later, the mystery of his disappearance is as baffling as ever.

WHAT REALLY HAPPENED?

For a long time it was thought that Fawcett had been murdered by tribespeople of the Upper Xingu River. But Fawcett took care to stay on friendly terms with local people and always took gifts for them. It is most likely that he simply got lost or died of natural causes in the jungle.

 The Mato Grosso region of Brazil has often been visited by explorers searching for lost cities.

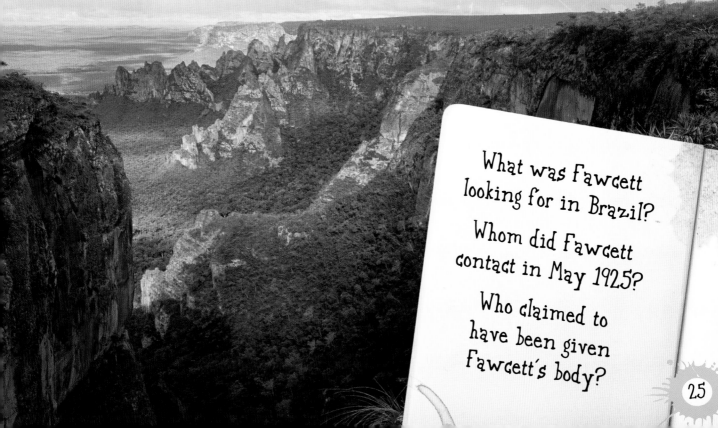

What was Fawcett looking for in Brazil?

Whom did Fawcett contact in May 1925?

Who claimed to have been given Fawcett's body?

Between 250 BCE and 900 CE, southern Mexico was home to one of the greatest civilizations the world has ever known. Then the huge stone buildings of the Mayan people mysteriously crumbled and their cities were reclaimed by the jungle. What happened?

DISAPPEARANCE FILE

Subject	Mayan Civilization
Date	780 CE onwards
Place	Southern Mexico
Status	UNEXPLAINED

 Mayan texts have been found inscribed on stone monuments and pottery. Some texts were also painted on a type of paper made from tree bark.

A THRIVING CIVILIZATION

Mayan civilization thrived for nearly 2000 years. The Mayans were great builders, mathematicians and scientists. From **observatories** like the one at Chichen Itza, they even tracked the movements of the planets. Then something happened that turned their world upside down.

From about 780 CE, the Mayan cities were suddenly abandoned. It was as if the inhabitants had left and never returned. When people learned to read Mayan symbols in the 1970s, experts hoped the inscriptions would explain what had happened. They did not.

FAMINE AND DROUGHT

The mysterious decline of the great Mayan civilization has always puzzled historians. Several Mayan cities have been excavated, but no signs of warfare or violent conflict have ever been found.

For a long time it was believed that a terrible sickness attacked the population, or that a disease killed off their crops and caused the people to starve. Recently, it has been suggested that the Mayans suffered a catastrophic drought that caused famine and loss of life on a huge scale.

The Kukulkan Pyramid at Chichen Itza is one of the most important surviving remnants of Mayan civilization. Like all Mayan structures, it was built by armies of labourers without the help of machines or metal tools.

WHAT REALLY HAPPENED?

It now seems very likely that a large-scale drought could have caused the sudden collapse of the Mayan world. Scientists have looked at soil samples taken from Mexico's Lake Chichancanab. These show that in the ninth century when Mayan civilization disappeared, the region was at its driest for 7000 years.

Where was the lost world of the Maya?

When did the Mayan civilization collapse?

When did people first learn to read Mayan symbols?

THE SHIP THAT WOULDN'T DIE

In the 1920s, the SS *Baychimo* was a small cargo steamer that sailed around the northern coast of Canada, delivering supplies and trading furs with local people. Then one cold day in 1931, the Arctic ice closed in. The *Baychimo* was trapped!

ARCTIC RESCUE

Realizing he and his crew were in danger, the captain radioed for help. Soon after, the first-ever **airlift** from the Arctic took place. Twenty-two of the ship's crew were rescued. The rest decided to shelter nearby for the winter and re-board the ship in the spring when the ice melted.

Since the *Baychimo* first drifted free of the ice, people have managed to board her several times, but nobody ever succeeded in rescuing her or towing her safely back to harbour.

DISAPPEARANCE FILE

Subject   *SS Baychimo*
Date   24 November 1931
Place   Arctic Ocean
Status   UNEXPLAINED

It never happened. After a severe blizzard in late November, the crew emerged from their wooden huts to find that the pack ice had loosened – and the *Baychimo* had floated away!

GHOST SHIP

Since then, the *Baychimo* has often been spotted drifting across the Arctic Ocean. In 1932, an explorer caught sight of her while sledding across the Arctic. The next year, Inuit hunters saw the ship and boarded her, but had to leave when they saw a storm approaching. In September 1935 and November 1939, the ship was spotted again near Wainwright, Alaska. In 1962, another group of Inuit people sighted her on the Beaufort Sea.

 Inuit people live throughout the Canadian and Arctic regions where the Baychimo has been seen.

The last recorded sighting was in 1969 – 38 years after the *Baychimo* had first been abandoned.

In the early 1990s, the company that originally owned the *Baychimo* was unable to say whether the little ship was still afloat. Perhaps she is still adrift somewhere in the Arctic....

WHAT REALLY HAPPENED?

The Arctic Ocean has a pattern of circular currents that are driven by wind and by oceanic flows. These flows come in via the Bering Straits and the Greenland Sea. Once the Baychimo was caught in these unpredictable currents, it could have drifted in and out of inhabited areas, ending up almost anywhere.

What type of ship was the Baychimo?

When was the Baychimo last seen?

When did the Baychimo first become trapped in the ice?

GLOSSARY

Airlift An operation to rescue people by plane or helicopter.

Altitude Height above sea level. On high mountains, climbers need breathing equipment to cope with the effects of altitude.

Aluminium A type of metal.

Analyze To examine something very carefully.

Baffling Hard to explain, puzzling.

Bizarre Strange or unusual.

Cairn A pile of stones built as a landmark or to mark a grave.

Cannibals Tribal people who eat the flesh of humans for food or as part of a ritual.

Cargo Goods carried on a ship.

Chief mate A senior officer on board a ship.

Colony A community of settlers.

Drought A time when there is no rain and crops do not grow well.

Enslave To force a person to work very hard without being paid.

Excavate To dig up remains of a civilization.

Famine A time when there is not enough food to eat.

Headland A piece of land that sticks out into the sea.

Hold The part of a ship where the cargo is stored.

Landing stage A place where a ship or boat can tie up safely.

Lifeboat A vessel that passengers and crew can use to escape from a sinking ship.

Lighthouse A tall building with a light at the top to guide ships at night.

Logbook A written record of events.

Myth (a) An ancient story, often about gods or heroes; (b) a story that is found not to be true.

Oasis A fertile area in the desert where water can be found.

Observatory A building from which scientists can study the night sky.

Oilskin A type of thick, waterproof jacket.

Ore Raw material from which metals can be extracted.

Plaque A memorial stone or plate.

Sandstorm A strong wind in a desert carrying clouds of sand.

Séance A meeting where people try to make contact with the spirits of dead people.

Settler A person who goes to start a new life in another country.

Spy A person who secretly tries to find out information.

Steamer A type of ship with a coal-fired engine.

Summit The highest point of a mountain.

Telegram A type of message that is sent by telephone wires but is delivered in printed form.

Torpedo A missile that travels through water and can be launched from the air

U-boat A German submarine.

Unstable Unbalanced, liable to tip over.

Wreckage Debris left after an accident or sinking.

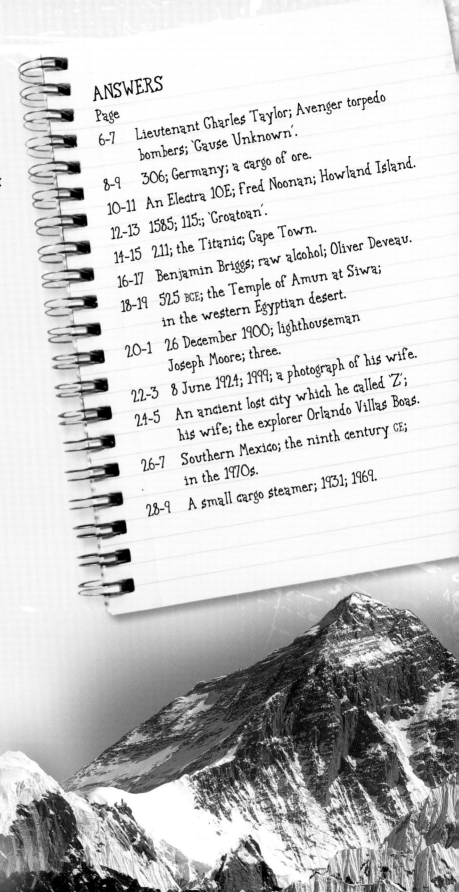

ANSWERS

Page

6-7   Lieutenant Charles Taylor; Avenger torpedo bombers; 'Cause Unknown'.

8-9   306; Germany; a cargo of ore.

10-11   An Electra 10E; Fred Noonan; Howland Island.

12-13   1585; 115:; 'Croatoan'.

14-15   211; the Titanic; Cape Town.

16-17   Benjamin Briggs; raw alcohol; Oliver Deveau.

18-19   525 BCE; the Temple of Amun at Siwa; in the western Egyptian desert.

20-1   26 December 1900; lighthouseman Joseph Moore; three.

22-3   8 June 1924; 1999; a photograph of his wife.

24-5   An ancient lost city which he called 'Z'; his wife; the explorer Orlando Villas Boas.

26-7   Southern Mexico; the ninth century CE; in the 1970s.

28-9   A small cargo steamer; 1931; 1969.

WEBSITES

http://www.ameliaearhart.com/
A site dedicated to the memory of Amelia Earhart.

http://www.byerly.org/bt.htm
A site about the many strange events that have taken place in the Bermuda Triangle.

http://www.maryceleste.net/
All about the mystery of the *Mary Celeste*.

Website information is correct at time of going to press. However, the publishers cannot accept liability for any information or links found on third-party websites.

INDEX